FATIMA VENTURA

Therapy with Jesus

a memoir & testimony

First edition

ISBN: 979-8-218-81409-0

This book was professionally typeset on Reedsy.
Find out more at reedsy.com

Contents

Introduction

I grew up in a traditional Mexican home, although we did not attend church, the acknowledgment of God was instilled in me at a young age. I remember praying to God about silly things, but my impression of God was more like a genie in a bottle. I was happy when things went my way, but I became bitter when they didn't.

I

Part One

2022

In 2022, I sought a greater purpose. I often asked, "What is my purpose? Why do I feel this void?" There had to be more to life than existing, but I was far from God and very much in the world. It was strange; I felt no pain, anger, or emotion. That numbness became my norm. Despite having status, a house, a car, a career, a family, a loving husband, and two daughters, a persistent void remained. I couldn't fill or understand it and drifted from emptiness to numbness.

I tried to fill the void with poor decisions, but religion was the one thing I refused. When people shared the Gospel, I avoided it. Talking to God felt like a one-way portal; I felt no connection. So, I turned to self-help books and motivational speakers. I tried manifestation and other coping methods, but nothing worked. Unhappy, I searched for logical reasons, blaming my job, husband, or environment. Eventually, I decided I was burnt out and needed time to reflect.

I had hit rock bottom physically, emotionally, and mentally—though pride kept me from admitting it. My pride hid my pain, and I refused to ask for help. I also had unresolved business with God, and it was time to talk. I didn't know this was the start of my journey, but with nothing left to lose, I finally moved from despair to hope and called out to Jesus.

I said, "Jesus, if you are real, help me figure myself out. I have tried on my own, but now I'm willing to follow your path. I just ask for wisdom and peace. I'm tired."

A few weeks later, I'd forgotten my plea to God, distracted by daily demands: kids, husband, bills, errands, work. As responsibilities mounted, guilt grew—especially about being a bad mom. Though I knew it wasn't true, the guilt weighed heavily, shifting me from distracted to burdened. By then, I had spent four years in law enforcement, and my job drained me. The graveyard shift, paperwork, absence from home, marital tension, and guilt from missing my daughters took a toll. When I was home, I was too tired to care. I felt overwhelmed, wanting to do everything on my own, even with a supportive husband. Both work and home life were demanding.

I wanted to find balance and handle everything. I loved my family and career, but I had built my whole identity around my job and couldn't imagine leaving something I had worked so hard to achieve. Independence was a point of pride—almost a form of self-idolization.

I was self-centered and found it hard to depend on anyone, even my husband. This mindset made me question how I could leave my job and provide for my family. Relying on others—especially those close to me—was difficult to accept.

Torment

During this time, rising police officer deaths weighed on me. A neighboring agency lost three officers in six months, and frequent End of Watch obituaries reminded me of the risks. Police ambushes and deaths became more common. Although this is a known risk—some say, "it's the nature of the beast"—these incidents made me reflect.

I often imagined myself in a coffin, leaving my daughters unable to understand my absence. This contemplation led me to reevaluate my life, family, and beliefs. Given my profession, one might expect me to have a strong faith, but that was not the case.

A recurring dream haunted me—a dream of death woke me up gasping. I didn't know if these dreams were fears or a message from above, but I sensed death was near. If it came, where did I stand with God? Was I saved? These questions made me realize I was on a self-destructive path and needed to reevaluate my priorities.

My Career & Resentment

I began my law enforcement career when my kids were a year and a half old. I felt a lot of guilt for not spending enough time with them. Balancing the demands of my early career and motherhood was a constant struggle that only grew more challenging.

When my twin daughters were almost two years old, I noticed they were missing some developmental milestones. I initially blamed their premature birth, but when I observed regression, I knew something was wrong. At three years old, my worst fears were confirmed—they were diagnosed with autism.

I couldn't understand why this was happening to me and my daughters. I found myself questioning God: "Why me? How could you do this?" I felt betrayed and wanted nothing to do with Him. I felt robbed— robbed of a normal experience. Blinded by anger, I believed I was being punished and forgotten. I pitied my children and resented the pity of others. It's hard to put into words the depth of this pain, but it created a rift between me and God.

My emotions overwhelmed me. With two daughters to care for, I questioned whether I was at fault. Was there something wrong with me? Was it genetic? Was it my husband's fault? Were we incompatible? The list of doubts seemed endless. I masked my emotions and dealt with my heartbreak in silence. Outwardly, I appeared strong and calm, even though I struggled to accept the situation.

From Many Questions to One

❧

I needed a break to figure things out, so I decided to leave my job. At first, I found myself with a lot of free time, which was quite uncomfortable. I was so used to being occupied that I didn't know what to do with myself. To help distract me, I started a home project: I hired a general contractor to convert my garage into an ADU unit. I wanted it to generate some rental income since I had decided to stay home for a while.

Things were going well, and I eventually developed a routine. I would get the twins ready for school, put them on the school bus, and then head to the gym. After that, I would return home and tackle various tasks around the house. During this time, I read many books to keep myself occupied. One day, as I finished reading a book, a thought struck me: Had I truly given Jesus a chance? I had always asked for things and expected answers from Him, but I never took the time to build a relationship with Him. After all, who typically does things for strangers? I realized that I had no relationship with God, yet I expected Him to listen to me while I blamed and resented Him.

My plea to God was slowly being answered, though I was oblivious to it at the time. I now understand that the Holy Spirit prompted those spontaneous thoughts to guide me on the right path.

The Bible

The next day, I ordered a King James Bible on Amazon, and honestly, I had no idea what I was getting myself into, but I felt like I had nothing to lose. So when I received the Bible, I said Okay, I am going to try to read this like any other book, beginning to end. However, as I navigated through the Bible, I felt as if I were trying to read a foreign language.

Nothing made sense, and it wasn't easy to understand. Often, I would fall asleep reading, but I was determined. I began watching testimonies on YouTube and listening to people talk about their faith in such great detail; however, I didn't understand it. They would say God speaks through the Bible and so on, but honestly, I would laugh at that possibility. Yet, a part of me wanted to see for myself, so I started to seek the truth.

It was an unusual season for me, and I felt isolated. I did not interact much with anyone. I was so used to chaos and loudness, but for the first time, life felt quiet, and no one bothered me. My husband would leave for work, and the girls would be at school.

2023

One night on June 7, 2023, I woke up from a dream. Although I don't recall much of it, I distinctly remember the names Solomon and Bethel. I wanted to go back to sleep, but those words kept me awake. It felt bizarre, yet I knew they were important, so I grabbed my iPhone and typed "Solomon and Bethel" into my notes. After that, I was able to fall back asleep.

The next day, I immediately recognized that what I had written down was significant. I looked in the Bible for answers and was struck by the importance of these words. At first, it startled me, but after that experience, I decided to start journaling.

That day, I wrote the following in my journal:

Bethel: A holy place, a church, the house of God.
   The site where Jacob slept and dreamed of angels ascending and descending a ladder (Genesis 28:19).
   Abraham built an altar to God in Bethel.
   Bethel is known as the gate of heaven and a place of worship.

Solomon:
The King of Israel, who built the first temple, was a wise and wealthy man.
His name means wisdom, peace, and friend of God.

Summary:
I will find peace and wisdom in the house of God, in a place of worship.

As I wrote my summary, I was amazed and also in disbelief. Perhaps it was a coincidence, but it didn't feel like it. I had asked God for wisdom and peace, and here He was showing me how to obtain it. From that day forward, God began a healing journey with me. It felt like I was attending therapy sessions.

The House Project

❦

One afternoon, I was distraught about the construction project on my property. The contractor failed to complete the project on the agreed-upon date, causing me numerous setbacks. I would reach out to the contractor, and he would say one thing and do another. There was a lot of inconsistency and no sense of urgency, so I decided to file a complaint against his license. He then contacted me to reach an agreement, but I no longer wanted to negotiate. I wanted to take legal action, and I had every avenue to screw him over like I felt he had done to me.

Ironically, I was reading 1 Corinthians 6 around the time this incident happened. The verse consists of Paul expressing how Christians should resolve their disputes with each other rather than in court, and I was baffled at the fact that I was reading this and going through a similar situation. But I wanted to sue this man; my pride was bigger than my logic.

A few days later, he knocked on my front door to propose an agreement, and while we conversed, he began to share about his personal life. He told me he had a child on the spectrum, a 13-year-old boy, and how difficult it was to manage a business and personal life. I knew exactly what he meant, although I didn't express that to him; I knew it as I was dealing with the same issues. We eventually reached an agreement, and I was able to see him in a different light; the project was completed with no further problems. That experience taught me how easy it is to love those we love, but, conversely, it is not so easy to love those who wrong us.

I consider this one of the first lessons: revenge produces no good fruit, and when I put it in God's hands, he blessed me abundantly. I ended up paying a lot less and had money left to remodel my kitchen, something I had longed to do.

A Dive Into My Youth

I continued to experience a series of events in which God pursued me and led me to a deeper understanding of myself. I refer to these events as a form of therapy with Jesus Christ.

Growing up, my father worked a lot. It is safe to say he was a workaholic; he also resembled a macho man. My father had an awful temper; he didn't drink or do drugs, but his temper was terrifying. He was very abusive, mainly towards my mother and oldest sister. I remember my father beating my mother on multiple occasions; in one specific incident, he dislocated her arm. I do not recall her going to the hospital, perhaps out of fear. Still, I do remember my mom's arm getting worse, and my dad eventually took her to a "Curandero," which is a traditional Mexican healer, to help adjust her arm back in place. However, to this day, my mother denies the severity of all the injuries my father would inflict on her, and for many years, this angered me.

My father was also unfaithful to my mother countless times, and I could not understand why my mother never left him. It was an endless cycle of physical and verbal abuse. I do not share this to judge my parents. I love them both unconditionally, but I am not oblivious to the fact that we were a dysfunctional family, and some things still surface within me that I had not allowed myself to process. Jesus was bringing these buried emotions to the surface and aiding me with his love and grace.

As God helped me digest my younger years, it became evident to me that a part of my childhood trauma had also influenced my marriage. I say that because my younger self never wanted to end up like my mother, I never wanted a man to control me or hurt me, and I never wanted to feel trapped due to financial necessities or children. I never wanted to feel vulnerable or be submissive to a man, and I did not want to go through what my mother went through, but in an attempt not to become like my mother, I became very much like my father.

Marriage

꧁꧂

I used to have a terrible temper, and unfortunately, it was often directed towards my husband. Reflecting on those years, I can see how self-centered I was. While I never engaged in physical abuse, I was verbally harsh and showed him little respect. I believed I was superior, forgetting that as spouses, we should function as a team. Any minor inconvenience would lead me to blame him and even to threaten divorce. Today, I am grateful for my husband's patience and for the fact that he never pursued the idea of separation. Looking back, I realize that this was only the beginning of our struggles, not the end.

As I healed through my traumas with God's help, I began to feel a deep conviction about my behavior and everything I had put my husband through. One evening, as I sat in our dimly lit living room, the soft glow of a lamp casting gentle shadows on the walls, a sense of urgency washed over me. I could hear the distant hum of our daughter's playing in their room, while the ticking of the clock in the background seemed to echo my racing thoughts. In my seven years of marriage (at that time), I had never been transparent or had a deep conversation with my husband. However, God began to present more opportunities for us to be honest with one another. We both had been occupied with life, trying to build something for our family, and in a sense, we had just fallen apart.

I also struggled with my daughter's diagnosis, and I felt like he did not understand my pain and desperation. My husband is not the type to vocalize his problems or worries, but God showed me that does not mean he does not care. We both loved our children very much, but we were dealing with the affliction differently.

I continued reading the bible, journaling, and playing worship music. I was growing in faith, and I was doing things I found out of character, like lifting my hands and singing songs of praise. In those moments, I felt an overpowering beauty, and nothing else mattered. It was as if my soul was reaching for something greater, a universal longing to be understood and uplifted by a presence larger than myself. I wanted to tell the world about the reality of Jesus Christ, but often I would shy away from talking about Him.

The Voices

O ne particular day, as I attempted to read the Bible, a spine-chilling feeling overcame me, and I began to hear voices. These voices would torment me, chanting "Satan, Satan" every time I attempted to read; they would interrupt me. The voices were not coming from me; they were not a part of my internal monologue, nor were they my inner conscious voice or anything like that.

Indeed, what I was experiencing was my first encounter with spiritual warfare. These evil entities were not pleased that I was seeking God, and they would torment me to the point where I did not want to read the Bible just to silence the noise in my head. I tried to pray the voices away, but quite frankly, I was terrified, and I would think, Have I gone mad? I had never experienced mental illness. If I told someone what I was going through, they would think mental illness was the case. If I told my husband, he would freak out. However, at some point, amidst the chaos, I made a pivotal decision. I decided that fear would not dictate my next step. I resolved to face the voices with courage, seeking strength in my faith and the power of Jesus Christ to rebuke the evil entities.

This series of events sounds insane out loud, and I was afraid no one would believe me, but I confided in my sister. I told her everything I was experiencing, and at first, she seemed skeptical, but having known me my entire life, she could see that I was not well. My sister advised me to continue to pray and seek God because I must be on the right path if I had pissed off the enemy.

My seeking a relationship with God erupted into a spiritual battle, and for nearly two weeks, I was tormented. I would hear the voices trying to interrupt me throughout the day, so I continued to rebuke them in the name of Jesus Christ. Terrified yet compelled, every time I said His name, I gathered more courage to confront whatever was haunting me. After those two intense weeks, I found peace, and I declare, 'I have never heard those voices again.' I thank God for His grace and glory. I have no doubt He was with me.

I was hesitant to write about this because such things sound crazy, but it is part of my testimony, and it also led my sister and me closer to God. Shortly after this experience, we discussed joining a church or seeking out active people in their faith, and I understood more than ever the importance of being in fellowship with other believers, because the enemy is actively engaged in his mission to steal, kill, and destroy.

John 10:10 - The thief comes only to steal and kill and destroy: I have come that they may have life, and have it to the full.

A Dream

⚜

One morning, I woke up from a dream that felt so real. I was inside a tomb cave, and I could see myself lying on my back on a large stone. I was completely undressed, and my body was covered in a white sheet. I could see myself covered in sweat, surrounded by people saying words over me. As they continued to speak, someone would hold a white cloth to dry the sweat off my forehead and shoulders. I had been petrified in the past by spiritual warfare, but this dream was the opposite of those feelings. I felt that I was healing from a sickness, and people were present, caring for me, which gave me a sense of comfort.

God continued to use people of faith to communicate with me. Whether it was a word, advice, or encouragement, I had never encountered so many people who openly discussed their faith or spoke passionately about God. I felt like these occurrences were intentional, as I usually had a question for God or thought about something, and the next thing I knew, I was conversing with people about that specific thought or question.

Sugar Bloom

A local coffee/bakery announced on Instagram that they would be having bible studies in their shop, and everyone was welcome. God's community found me before I could find a church. I told my sister about it, and we began attending these bible groups. At first, I believed my sister had joined just to show me moral support. However, as we continued attending, I witnessed how God began to move in her heart. We were both very new to our faith, but I was thrilled she was there with me, and we were both seeking God and biblical knowledge.

Throughout this season, I continued to have vivid dreams and felt spiritually in tune.

While attending Bible studies, I met a lady who was about my age, and one day she asked me if I wanted to meet her at the coffee shop and hang out. At first, I was a little hesitant because I hadn't known her long, and I didn't want to be pressured about joining a church or anything like that, but I agreed to meet with her. During our coffee meeting, she told me a little bit about herself and what God was doing in her life. She also shared with me that she had a daughter in a different country whom she had not been able to see for some time, as she was in the process of regularizing her immigration status.

I could not imagine going through a situation where I couldn't be with my children," I added, and then I told her about my 6-year-old daughters and how I was having a difficult time accepting their situation. I was new in my walk with Jesus, and I didn't understand many things. She acknowledged my concerns and validated my emotions, as she was also going through a situation over which she had no control.

She then told me that sometimes we have to surrender those situations to God. In other words, entrust him with your daughters' situation. When she said this, I knew all she was saying was essentially the right thing to do, but I didn't know how to put it into practice. I considered it practically impossible for me to give it all to God. I didn't know how to completely surrender to the emotions of fear, worry, and impatience.

One evening, after much reflection and the encouragement of my new friend, I found myself kneeling beside my bed after tucking the girls in. I whispered a simple prayer, 'God, I can't carry this alone. I trust you with my daughters' future. Help me find peace in your plan.' With that small act, I felt a slight release, a path forward, an illustration of surrender that I could cling to whenever doubt tried to seep back in.

Small but Mighty

⚜

One morning, my daughter Aloni was unwell, so she stayed home from school, and we planned a trip to the nutrition store. While getting ready, she locked our house key in my room; fortunately, she had detached my car key from the key chain, and I was still able to get to the car. On our way to the store, I questioned whether my spiritual experiences meant anything or if I was just a desperate mother. I wished for a sign from God, asking him to let me see a hummingbird if He was truly with me, though I doubted it would happen. Aloni and I went inside the store and enjoyed our favorite beverage.

When we arrived home, Aloni wanted to play in the backyard, and she ran to her swing, but it was a cold morning, and she was a bit congested, so I said, "No, Aloni, we are going inside." I walked towards her, but she was actively swinging, so I sat down on our trampoline and gave her a few minutes to swing.

While waiting for her, I heard a loud buzzing sound. I looked towards the noise and noticed my orange tree was covered in bees. They were buzzing so rapidly that the more I focused on them, the louder I heard their pitching hum. I found this very odd. I had seen bees there before, but what I was witnessing was an abundance of bees; all of the orange blossoms were completely covered. Amazed, I lay on the trampoline and stared at my bee-infested tree when out of nowhere, a thought came to mind, "Just like the bees are buzzing, your prayers are buzzing in heaven". I stopped for a second and said Wow, what was that? That's very poetic. I don't even think like that, but my goodness, could it be that God had finally heard or acknowledged my prayer? By this time, Aloni had gotten off the swing, and as I hopped off the trampoline to grab her, I looked to my left, and there it was: a tiny hummingbird flying in place, small but mighty, making sure I captured its presence. With tears rushing down my face, I was in awe, and I said God, thank you, let them be a constant reminder that you are with me.

God knows I cannot make such things up, and from that day forward, truly I tell you, I have seen so many hummingbirds on multiple occasions that I have lost count.

Part-time Job

I n August 2023, I took on a part-time job as a special education tutor at a middle school to learn more proactive ways to support my daughters and ultimately understand the services the school district provided. I wanted to be involved and learn as much as I could. The classroom I was assigned to had about 12 students with severe disabilities, including learning disabilities, ADHD, Autism, Down syndrome, nonverbal communication barriers, and other medical conditions. My daughters were much younger than the students I was caring for, and seeing that the students were more severely affected than my daughters filled me with sadness. However, I also experienced a sense of appreciation for my circumstances, knowing it could have been worse. As I continued to work with the students and build a rapport with them, I began to see them for their abilities rather than their disabilities. This experience taught me to do the same with my daughters. Previously, I focused on what I feared my girls lacked: words they struggled to pronounce, social cues they missed, or milestones they hadn't achieved. Now, I celebrate what they can do: the smiles they share, the laughter that fills our home, and their unique ways of understanding the world. It was in their strengths that I found a new appreciation and love.

In this season, I became very in tune with my emotions; quite frankly, I became very emotional. The students were so pure-hearted and tender that they had no idea how much they helped me heal. One particular interaction stands out in my memory. There was a student named Jessie, who was very active and kept all the adults on their toes. One afternoon, Jessie came over to me during a quiet moment and handed me a hand-drawn picture, along with a chocolate bar wrapped in a white Christmas wrapper, and he said softly, 'This is for you. I love you, Ms. Patina. Merry Christmas." Instantly, tears welled up in my eyes. It was a simple gesture, yet it broke through a personal barrier I didn't realize I had. This small act of connection embodied so much love and hope, and it was in moments like these that I truly understood the significance of their impact on me. God used these interactions to change my perspective and give me hope. I needed them more than they needed me.

As I was relatively new to the job, I was assigned a specific mentor to teach me and help me gain on-the-job experience. However, this trainer did not get along with the other employees in my classroom, so she withdrew, and we only spoke briefly. I was initially upset, but later realized it was not personal, as God had someone else in mind for me.

I was assigned a different mentor, and we met weekly on Mondays on my campus. I still remember the first time I met her. As she walked towards me in her long pink dress, she radiated a welcoming smile, and at that moment, I just knew that whatever was going on here, God was involved. We greeted each other and walked to the classroom. It was a late start for the students, so we had the classroom to ourselves. Ironically, when we started talking and getting to know each other, she did not shy away from being a Christian. I immediately thought, God, you are so funny and intentional.

She proceeded to speak about her upbringing and shared her testimony with me. I also talked about the things I was going through, and I began to cry in front of this stranger. It was pretty embarrassing. I had just met this lady, and here I was in tears; a part of me did not recognize my actions. It was not like me to show vulnerability or my emotions, but I knew whatever was happening was bigger than me. Although I felt very comfortable, such an experience was foreign to me. After that day, we continued meeting on Mondays, and our meetings consisted of Jesus Christ, and she mentored me in faith. It is incredible to see how the things of God work. I'm not sure if she knew God had sent her on a short assignment to mentor me spiritually, but I was grateful for it.

A STILL WHISPER

~❦~

O ne night, my daughter Aloni had trouble sleeping. This was common as she would go through cycles where she would sleep well, and other times she would battle with insomnia. But that night, I was quite exhausted trying to keep her from running in and out of the room. She would persistently run down the hallway, and I had to get out of bed and grab her. Although I would doze off here and there, I couldn't fall asleep, uneasy about the fact that Aloni would unlock the doors, climb on cabinets, or leave water running.

Around one in the morning, I was fed up with having to get out of bed. For the last time, I went down the hallway and screamed, "Aloni, why can't you just F***** Listen!" As the last word left the tip of my tongue, I instantly heard a voice say, "How do you think I feel every time I have to go back and get you?" I stood still for a second, knowing what I had heard didn't come from my internal monologue. In disbelief, I simply smirked and murmured to myself, "Man, I must be tired."

The next morning, like any other day, I woke up and got the girls ready for school. I then left for the gym and started my cardio on the stair master. While I was still adjusting the StairMaster settings, I felt an authoritative presence hover over me. I cannot quite explain it, but I instantly remembered what had happened the night before, and it dawned on me that God had spoken to me, and I had ignored Him. I tried to control my tears but inevitably failed. I was so embarrassed that people would approach me to see if I was OK. So I said Jesus, if this is you, please let me get out of here, and we can just talk in the comfort of my home. I then took a deep breath, stopped the stair master, and sprinted out of the gym.

Full of conviction, I rushed home, processing what I had heard the night before. "How do you think I feel every time I have to go back and get you? I was astonished; I never imagined I would experience such things. God spoke to me, and he gave me a perfect analogy to understand how frustrated he was with me.

I walked into my home, and I completely broke down in tears. I did not know what to say to God. I was terrified as I knew God had spoken to me, and I was a sinner. So I walked into my room, sat on the edge of my bed, and wept! After some time, I was able to compose myself, and I said to God I am so sorry. I then said the sinner's prayer and agreed to accept Jesus Christ as my Lord and Savior (I had only learned about the sinner's prayer from watching De La Fe testimonies on YouTube).

I felt so small and dispirited about the way I had been, and to know that God had not given up on me was a profound feeling. So I sat there contemplating my life when suddenly I felt the need to bow my head and shut my eyes. As I did, an overwhelming sense of warmth enveloped me, as if a gentle embrace held me close. A sensation of brightness filled the room, not of sight but of pure energy. It moved towards me, and the closer it got, the more I wept uncontrollably. My heart pounded with a vivid aliveness, and I felt a sense of renewal coursing through my entire being. Love, shelter, forgiveness, and peace washed over me in a wave so tangible that it both humbled and lifted me. As this divine presence slowly began to drift away, it left me reassured, surrounded by a deep sense of love.

After this experience, I was content. God is real! !! and no one told me, "no religious folk", not a church... I experienced it. This truly marked the most profound and greatest experience in my life.

Seeing the Spectrum of Wonder

❦

One day, my daughters were playing in our backyard, and I was in awe, embracing their growth and the joy of their laughter. Aliyah loves to dance and sing. She began to speak around the age of five, and although she is very emotional and struggles with coping with her feelings, she has improved so much socially. Aloni enjoys being barefoot and swinging on the playground swing. She is nonverbal but is very persistent in getting my attention. My girls are my most precious possessions, and I am filled with gratitude for their existence.

Later that night, the gratitude I felt began to shift subtly into fear. The weight of the day's joy turned into anxious thoughts that made my heart race. My mind wandered to Aliyah. Would other kids welcome her quirks with warmth, or would her sensitive nature lead to tears if things got overwhelming? Then my concerns turned to Aloni's first day of school, picturing her struggling to communicate her needs and feeling frustrated. These specific scenarios created a vivid sense of vulnerability, stirring a deep-seated anxiety within me. Every parent desires the best for their children, and I worried about their protection and acceptance by the world. I didn't immediately understand why these thoughts surfaced, but their intensity made me realize how deeply I wanted to shield my kids from adversity.

As I lay in bed, weighed down by these emotions, my feelings began to shift again. With my eyes closed but very much awake, I felt Jesus comfort me, offering a perspective beyond my anxieties. I saw the image of my daughter Aloni, as if I were seeing through her lens. Everything outdoors appeared vibrant and colorful. I could hear the sounds of the birds, louder than usual. I sensed the weight of a leaf falling and felt the wind brushing through my face as she swung back and forth on the swing. I felt the cool grass touching the bottom of her bare foot; it calmed me, and its cold sensation traveled through my spine. I was in a state of happiness and harmony, contrasting sharply with my earlier fears.

Then, as my reflections deepened, my perspective shifted. I saw an image of Aliyah and felt her genuine and intense love for humanity, as well as her ability to discern the emotions of others. I experienced her pure, innocent heart, joy, contentment, and passion for singing and making others laugh. Moving from anxiety to awe, I realized how witnessing these moments in my daughters' lives filled me with profound gratitude.

I invite you, dear reader, to consider the wonder in your own life: where it resides, how it manifests, and who in your life embodies it. Because of this experience, I encountered my savior; in my weakness, hurt, and sorrow, I saw how much my daughter's Autism led me to God—something I used to consider a punishment I now see as a blessing.

2024

I n March 2024, I decided to leave my job at school.   This decision stemmed from the changing needs in our household, as I needed to adjust my schedule to accommodate my girls' various appointments, including speech therapy, occupational therapy, ABA therapy, and transportation. Additionally, my husband was getting ready to attend a trade school. He was very excited about it, and I wanted to be flexible. The transition from working at school to being home again brought a new dynamic; my relationship with God felt stable, maybe even stronger than it had ever been. This shift felt like part of a greater surrender to God's plans, trusting that aligning my life with my family's needs was a step guided by faith, just as my previous decisions had been.

I recall a particular day when I had a tug at my heart. I felt the need to pray. I kept feeling this urge until I finally gave in and agreed to do so. For two weeks, I woke up early, around five in the morning. At the time, I didn't know why I had to do this or what to pray about, but I remained obedient, and I would wake up early. The first days were difficult. I would place my phone far away so I could get out of bed, and after some time and a strong cup of coffee, I was able to wake up before my alarm clock. Sometimes I would sit in silence, while at other times I would open my Bible app, read the verse of the day, or read a devotional, and sometimes I would pray about whatever came to mind.

Trails & Tribulations

W ell, shortly after I completed the two weeks of prayer, I realized why it was so vital for me to pray. God was preparing me for a season that would require much more of me. On April 10, 2024, my brother Jesus, the youngest of my siblings (17 years old), was admitted to the Loma Linda Hospital Intensive Care Unit, where he was hospitalized for nearly two months. My brother was given multiple diagnoses, and one of those diagnoses was a blood infection that caused three aneurysms in his intestines. These aneurysms were blocking the proper blood flow and were at risk of bursting at any moment. Hearing this news, I was overwhelmed with a profound sense of disbelief and grief, unable to comprehend how such adversity could strike someone so young.

The news devastated my entire family. We did not understand why this was happening; my brother was so young, and I thought, Why would God allow this to happen? I felt hopeless and confused. While at the hospital, my brother continued to get worse. He developed blood clots that caused internal bleeding on the left side of his brain, provoking a stroke. The stroke temporarily paralyzed his body, and the doctors had no answers for us. They mentioned a possible surgery, but were not confident about the outcome. The best-case scenario would be that my brother survives the surgery, but a large portion of his intestines would be removed, and he would receive nutrition through liquids for the rest of his life.

My family and I were living a nightmare; nothing like this had occurred to us before, and we kept receiving bad news after bad news. After about a month and a half, the doctors called a family meeting. They wanted to inform us that there was nothing they could do for my brother and that their priority had shifted to simply easing Jesus's pain. They pulled my parents aside and advised them to prepare for future arrangements.

This was a lot; I had trouble coping with it all, and witnessing my brother in excruciating pain was one of life's worst experiences. But I refused to accept that fate for my brother. Desperate and with nowhere to turn, I ran to God! I begged him to save my brother. I cried out, 'Please, Lord, let him wake tomorrow, let him find strength in his body to fight this battle.' My prayers were raw and urgent. I told him, 'Even if it is his time, Lord, I have faith that you can change it around, just as you gave King Hezekiah 15 more years of life after the prophet Isaiah told him he would die.' (Isaiah 38). I spoke to God, but I felt like God wasn't talking back to me. This caused me great sorrow, but I remained intentional about my request, knowing that God was bigger than the situation. I said to God, 'The doctors are helpless.' Let it be your hands that save my brother. Let this be a miracle in which no one can deny your divine existence.

A few more weeks passed, and I was back and forth at the hospital; sometimes, I would stay overnight so that my parents could go home and rest. I began to fast secretly for my brother's well-being. I mean,

I did everything I could think of. I was exhausted and sleep-deprived, but I did not care; I knew that what my brother was going through was much worse. Plus, I had a relationship with God now, and he had given me so many personal experiences that I refused to give up my faith at the first inconvenience I faced.

Hospital Visitations

⚬⚭⚬

During this season, my family was not close. My sisters and I had been estranged from our parents way before Jesus was hospitalized. We did not have the best relationship with our brother either, and the fact that he lived with our parents created more distance. At first, the encounters with my parents at the hospital were difficult to endure. There were numerous family issues and pride involved. I cannot speak for my sisters, but as for myself, I resented my parents for many reasons that I felt were justified. Looking back on life from my adult perspective, I can no longer understand many things that transpired during my childhood.

But I kept praying for a miracle, and often I was sad and discouraged. However, I would always return to my tangible experiences with God, and my spirit would be lifted. A lot of my family members looked at me as if I were crazy. How could she pretend everything was going to be okay? Since when is she all holy? Also, it did not help that I confronted my mother.

I confronted my mother about things the bible states are not okay. My mom was known to go to mediums and fortune tellers, and I knew she strongly desired to reunite our family. She had recently returned from a trip to Mexico, and I felt that perhaps she consulted with these mediums. So I told her that if she did something or inquired about something from these people, it was biblically wrong, and she needed to speak to God about it because my brother's life was at stake. My mom was furious that I dared to confront her, but she denied doing so, and we simply left it at that. As you can imagine, I heard all sorts of things from my family after that conversation, but for the sake of my brother, I remained cordial. I understood that you cannot fight evil with evil, so I tried to reflect good, loving, and humble characteristics. Plus, no matter how dysfunctional we were, I loved my family.

Slowly, I began to see nurses and other hospital personnel minister to my family. I even witnessed a doctor leading my brother in the sinner's prayer, and my brother accepting Jesus Christ as his lord and Savior. Although this was such a difficult time, it was beautiful to see God's presence in the midst of it all. It was a quiet evening when, amidst the hum of the hospital monitor, I took a deep exhale. In that moment, my desperate prayers transformed into a serene calmness that enveloped me. I was covered in peace that surpassed all understanding. I just knew my brother was going to be okay. Although nothing had changed with his condition, I began to see how God was allowing this experience to serve a greater good.

My brother slowly began to recover without the need of surgery, and his time in the hospital allowed my family to speak and settle many things we would have otherwise never spoken of. After three long months, my brother returned home, and today, he is enjoying his young adult life, healthy and in good spirits. My relationship with my parents has also improved.

My Inner Dealings

⚜

While my brother was at the hospital, I had a dream where someone spoke to me. The voice was calm and reassuring, carrying a warmth that seemed to cover me despite not seeing the person it belonged to. I heard, "Why don't you accept this gift?" In that dream, I was not told what the gift was, but somehow I knew what the voice was referring to. It was referring to a child. At first, I was hesitant, but then I replied, "I accept this gift, but how do I know this is real, or how do I know this is from God, and what will I name it?" And then I heard, "Able, for God is Able." Immediately, I woke up. I said, "A baby?" I was not trying to conceive, nor did I want to; I believed that this was God telling me He was able to do all things, like heal my brother, my children, and so on. For days, I reflected on my dream, and as I examined the words "for God is able," it was a very open-ended statement that God has no limitations; he is God.

About three weeks later, I discovered that I was indeed pregnant, and I was thrilled to share the news with my family. I was sure that all would go well with my pregnancy because I had this vivid dream and considered the pregnancy a gift from god.

However, when I turned 7 weeks, I began to bleed. At first, it was very light, and I did not think much of it. But as the bleeding progressed and cramping began, I decided to go to the ER. I was so confused. Why is this happening? The doctor confirmed I was having a miscarriage and that there was nothing I could do other than go home and try to rest. I returned home and, the following day, continued to experience contractions. I felt a sense of helplessness as I lay on my bedroom floor in a fetal position, screaming in pain. In that moment, I paused and questioned the fairness of it all, but I also searched within for a sense of calm acceptance, acknowledging that some things are beyond our control.

Eventually, my husband helped me to our bathroom and sat me on the toilet, and there I felt my womb empty. I saw a little piece of me, about the size of my thumb, floating in the toilet water. I cried out loud, 'This is what I get.' I was not angry with God; this time, I was furious with myself. It was only at that moment that I understood that only God can give life and take it away.

Before I started my walk with God, I found myself unexpectedly expecting a child. At that time, life was overwhelming. My career was demanding, and I felt stretched thin by the responsibilities of motherhood and work. The timing felt impossible, and I made the difficult decision to have an abortion, choosing not to share this with my husband. In those moments, I felt a desperate need to keep things manageable and vaguely hoped that a future moment would offer more clarity. I justified it to myself, saying I was already so occupied with my daughters and work that I could not manage another child. I now look back with compassion for that version of me, understanding the pressures and fears that led to that decision, even as I process its weight.

My appointment for that abortion was fast; they gave me a pill at Planned Parenthood, and about two hours later, I began bleeding. During that time, I did question if I was doing the right thing, but the thought didn't go further than that. Now, I think back on the women sitting in that same waiting room I was in, and I wonder how many of us carry silent stories of uncertainty and regret. In this moment of reflection, I began to understand that God's discipline was not a punishment but a guiding light towards a renewed purpose. Through acceptance of His correction, I found a path to healing and hope.

I sat on the toilet and grieved my miscarriage and the other baby I robbed of life, a hard pill to swallow, but God is a fair God, a God of justice, and his discipline and correction are an act of love. I had done something wrong, and I needed to take responsibility for it.

Hebrews 12:6 for the lord disciplines those he loves, and he punishes each one he accepts as his children.

As I reflect on my life experiences, I realize that our shared experiences of grappling with difficult choices and unexpected outcomes resonate deeper within the human experience. What future stories sat unspoken between us—each of us silently navigating our own seas of doubt and hope? It is in these moments of collective searching that we find a communal bond, an understanding that the journey through pain and purpose connects more than just our individual paths but defines our shared humanity. Through this lens, I see my path to healing and hope as intertwined with those of others, our lives guided by faith, resilience, and a quest for deeper meaning.

Healing Process

‿᪥᪥‿

Through raw conversations with Jesus Christ, I have learned to know and understand myself better. I have allowed myself to sit with my feelings and not suppress everything. Jesus has walked me through the most vulnerable areas of my life, allowing me to feel without judgment, and has rewired my brain to think differently and heal.

Before deepening our faith, my husband and I often struggled with communication, and our conflicts would linger unresolved. However, with God at the center, we have found a new way to communicate openly and forgive quickly, rather than letting hurt fester and linger. For instance, we now dedicate time each evening to share our thoughts and pray together, which has fostered a deeper connection and understanding between us. Having been together for nearly a decade, we have learned that putting God at the center of our marriage and home is essential for a healthy and firm foundation.

I have witnessed the changes within myself and those around me, and the tangible presence of God is undeniable. He continues to uplift me.

This life and place are temporary; what's to come is eternal. Seek the truth, read your Bible & invite Jesus Christ into your heart.

I'm still in Therapy

∼⟨◦⟩∼

I am far from perfect, but I have God's love, light, grace, and peace to guide me. My circumstances have not changed entirely, but Jesus has changed my perspective; a relationship with him has given me new hope. I now walk confidently knowing that my identity is in Christ. Surrendering is a process, but be at peace. God's love is eternal, and He goes before us and beside us, directing our steps into His divine plan and purpose. As I continue my therapy sessions with Jesus, I invite you to seek a relationship with him. Start by taking a moment of quiet time to whisper a simple prayer, asking for guidance and understanding. May this story spark your first honest conversation with God.

Life is a journey, and my story continues. What was meant to break me, God has redeemed for His glory.

I hope my testimony touches you and the hearts of many. As I conclude this section, I envision a sunrise casting its warm glow over a horizon, symbolizing the dawn of new beginnings and endless possibilities. The sunrise, like a cherished gift, reminds us of the hope and renewal embedded within each day. Just as the first light of day brings hope and redemption, my journey exemplifies the promise of brighter tomorrows. In this moment of reflection, I remember the words from my dream—' Able, for God is Able'—underlining the limitless potential within our lives. May this image of sunrise bless you and inspire you to seek your own path to peace and a relationship with the Savior of the world, Jesus Christ.

Afterword

Ask, Seek, Knock

"Ask and it will be given to you; seek and you will find; knock and the door will be opened to you. For everyone who asks receives; the one who seeks finds; and to the one who knocks, the door will be opened."
Matthew 7:7-8